FAMOUS MINNESOTANS

Past and Present

Dan Flynn

NODIN PRESS

To my parents
Terry and Kathy Flynn

John Toren, Editor

Julie Tilka, Designer

Tom Van Asch, Photo Retouch

ISBN - 1-932472-29-0

Nodin Press is a division of Micawbers, Inc.
530 N. Third Street, Suite 120
Minneapolis, Minnesota 55401

Contents

Photo Credits

Front Cover: (Charles Lindbergh), Time Life Pictures, Getty Images; (Bob Dylan), Getty Images; (Kevin Garnett), Amanda Edwards, Getty Images; (Judy Garland), Eric Carpenter, Getty Images; Back Cover; (Garrison Keillor), James Keyser, Twin Images, Time Life Pictures, Getty Images; (Lea Thompson), Frederick M. Brown, Getty Images.

Author Photo: Joe Treleven

The Actors: p.2 (Judy Garland), MGM Studios Getty Images; p.4 (Lea Thompson), Ron Wolfson, Time Life Pictures, Getty Images; p.5 (Kevin Sorbo), Getty Images; p.6 (Josh Hartnett), Kevin Winter, Getty Images; p.7 (Rachael Leigh Cook), courtesy of Rachael Leigh Cook; p.9 (Al Franken), Al Hawthorne, Getty Images; p.10 (Lew Ayers), Hulton Archives, Getty Images; p.11 (Jane Russell), John Kobal Foundation, Getty Images; p.12 (Marion Ross), courtesy of Marion Ross; p.13 (Louie Anderson), courtesy of Louie Anderson; p.15 (Jessica Lange), Carlos Alvarez, Getty Images; p.16 (Peter Graves), Getty Images; p.17 (James Arness), Getty Images; p.18 (Tippi Hedren), courtesy of the Roar Foundation; p.19 (Cheryl Tiegs), Rob Rich, Getty Images; p.20 (The Coen Brothers), AP World Wide; p.21 (Winona Ryder), AP World Wide; p.23 (Terry Gilliam) , courtesy of Terry Gilliam; p.24 (Cedric Adams), courtesy of W.C.C.O.; p.25 (Arlene Dahl), Terry Fincher, Getty Images; p.26 (Eddie Albert), Hulton Archive, Getty Images; p.27 (Robert Vaughn), Hulton Archive, Getty Images; p.28 (Richard Dean Anderson), courtesy of Richard Dean Anderson; p.29 (Loni Anderson), AP World Wide.

The Civic Leaders: p.30 (Warren Burger) Minnesota Historical Society; p.32 (Harry Davis), courtesy of Harry Davis; p.33 (Roy Wilkins), Francis Miller, Time Life Pictures, Getty Images; p.35 (Hubert Humphrey), Minnesota Historical Society; p.36 (James Colby), Time Life Pictures, Getty Images; p.37 (Harry Blackmun), Dianna Walker, Time Life Pictures; p.38 (Elmer Anderson), courtesy of Nodin Press; p.40 (Paul Wellstone), Judy Griesedieck, Time Life Pictures, Getty Images; p.41 (Eugene McCarthy), Leonard McCombe, Time Life Pictures, Getty Images; p.42 (Harold Stassen), Hank Walker, Time Life Pictures, Getty Images; p.45 (Walter Mondale), Yvonne Hemsey, Getty Images.

The Athletes: p.46 (Kevin Garnett), David Sherman, N.B.A.E. via Getty Images; p.48 (Kirby Puckett), Ken Levine, Getty Images; p.49 (Paul Molitor), Bill Hickey, Getty Images; p.51 (Herb Brooks), Bruce Bennett, Getty Images; p.52 (Neal Broten), Focus on Sport, Getty Images; p.53 (Phil Housley), All Sport, Getty Images; p.54 (Brianna Scurry), Eric Lesser, Getty Images; p.55 (Tony Sanneh), courtesy of Tony Sanneh; p.56 (Tom Lehman), Ezra Shaw, Getty Images; p.57 (Patty Berg), Becker Fox Photo, Getty Images; p.59 (Alan Page), Minnesota Historical Society; p.60 (Tom Malchow), Hanish Blair, All Sport Getty Images; p.61(Greg Lemond), Tony Duffy, All Sport, Getty Images; p.62 (Harmon Killebrew), MLB via Getty Images; p.63 (Roger Maris), Herb Sharfman, Time Life, Getty Images; p.64 (Bronko Nagurski), Hulton Archive, Getty Images; p.65 (Vern Gagne), Minnesota Historical Society; p.67 (Dave Winfield), Jeff Haynes, AFP, Getty Images; p.68 (John Madden), Rick Stewart, Getty Images; p.69 (Bud Grant), Minnesota Historical Society; p.70 (Charles Bender), MLB Baseball via Getty Images; p.62 (George Mikan), NBAE via Getty Images; p.63 (Kevin McHale), Dale Trait NBAE via Getty Images.

The Scientists: p.70 (The Mayos), courtesy of the Mayo Clinic; p.72 (Peter Agre), courtesy of The John Hopkins University; p.73 (Dr. C. Walton Lillehei), Al Fenn, Time Life Pictures, Getty Images; p.75 (Sister Elizabeth Kenny), George E. Luxton, Minnesota Historical Society; p.76 (Norman Borlaug), Art Rickerby, Time Life Pictures, Getty Images; p.77 (Phillip Hench and Edward Kendall), courtesy of the Mayo Clinic.

The Writers: p.78 F. (Scott Fitzgerald), Hulton Archive, Getty Images; p.80 (Harrison Salisbury), Carl Mydans, Time Life Pictures, Getty Images; p.81 (Eric Sevareid), Stedman Jones, Time Life Pictures, Getty Images; p.83 (Garrison Keillor), Robin Platzer, Twin Images, Time Life Pictures, Getty Images; p.85 (Robert Bly), Per Breiehagen Time Life Pictures, Getty Images; p.88 (Sinclair Lewis), E.O. Hoppe, Time Life Pictures, Getty Images; p.86 (Louise Erdrich), Keri Pickett, Time Life Pictures, Getty Images; p.86 (August Wilson), Rex Rystedt, Time Life Pictures, Getty Images; p.91 (Sigurd Olson), Minnesota Historical Society.

The Business Leaders: p.92 (Curt Carlson), courtesy of the Carlson Companies; p.94 (Mike Wright), Bill Alkofer, courtesy of St. Thomas Academy; p.96 (Earl Baken), Sara Nealy, courtesy of Medtronic; p.97 (Rose Totino), courtesy of Joanne Elwell; p.99 (James J. Hill), Getty Images; p.100 (William Norris), courtesy of The William Norris Institute and The University of St. Thomas; p. 102 William McKnight, courtesy of 3M; p.103 (I.A. O'Shaughnessy), courtesy of the Department of Special Collections University of St. Thomas; p.105 (James Ford Bell), Minnesota Historical Society; p.106 (Carl Pohlad), courtesy of Carl Pohlad.

The Musicians: p.108 (Bob Dylan), Andrew DeLory, Hulton Archive, Getty Images; p.111 (The Andrews Sisters), Getty Images; p.112 (Prince), Frank Micelotta, Getty Images, p.114 (Lester Young), Ronald Startup, Getty Images; p.118 (Dominique Argento), courtesy of Bruce Carlson and The Schubert Theatre; p.117 (James Harris and Terry Lewis), Frederick M. Brown, Getty Images; p.118 (Yanni), Tim Boyle, Newsmakers, Getty Images; p.119 (The Replacements), Allen Beaulieu Photography.

The Explorers: p.120 (Charles Lindbergh), Minnesota Historical Society; p.122 (Will Steger), Phil Schofield, Time Life Pictures, Getty Images; p.123 (Ann Bancroft), Keri Pickett, Time Life Pictures, Getty Images.

The Artists: p.124 (Charles Schulz), Walter Daran, Time Life Pictures, Getty Images; p.126 (Warren Mackenzie), courtesy of Warren Mackenzie; p.127 (The Hautman Brothers), courtesy of The Hautman Brothers; p.128 (Wanda Gag), Robert Janssen, The Minnesota Historical Society; p.130 (LeRoy Neiman), Arnaldo Magnani, Getty Images; p.132 (Gordon Parks), Gordon Parks, Minnesota Historical Society.

Reasonable efforts were made to reach the photographers who have not been mentioned.

Foreword

PEOPLE WHO CALL THEMSELVES MINNESOTANS ARE A RATHER MODEST POPULATION. We were raised by elders who admonished us to never get too big for our britches. So we, instead, developed a pride of place. Winters here are worse than almost anywhere else in the country, and we are proud of that. It is allowed. Our own parents bragged about it. But there is another manner in which to show licit pride, and that is to point out, at appropriate times, famous people who also have called this place home.

It is helpful to those of us who sometimes fear that really important people think Minnesota is only farms and lakes and the Mall of America to point out that Hercules is from Mound, Minnesota. It has always been of some value to mention Lindbergh and Judy Garland, but as time passes, fewer people respond with gasps. However, the mention of Prince, in the same company, may get the job done. I once had a teenager in Seattle wish my autograph because I came from the same state as Josh Hartnett. I quite proudly obliged.

Famous Minnesotans gives us all bragging rights. This book will fill dull evenings at cocktail parties with hours of facts about famous people who come from the same place you do. And people will admire you. I recommend that you not only read, but memorize the text accompanying the pictures herein. Commit these facts to memory so that you may be inconspicuous in fine company from somewhere else until someone mentions Arlene Dahl, and you say, "She used to live just down the street from me."

The more you memorize, the more opportunities you'll have to feel good about being from Minnesota. You will be quiet, casually enjoying the company, hoping someone will bring up the Nobel Prize, and you drolly recollect that Phillip Hench and E.C. Kendall isolated cortisone and grabbed the prize in 1950 at the Mayo Clinic. "Oh, and by the way, did I mention the Mayo brothers?"

If I had some money, I would invite myself to the American Bar Association's next meeting and hang around at mixers. Sooner or later, someone would bring up Supreme Court Justice Harry Blackmun or Chief Justice Warren Burger, and I would nonchalantly say, "They are from Minnesota...grew up not too far from me."

Because the book organizes the famous by category — actors, civic leaders, athletes, scientists and more — there is no end to ways this book can give us a boost. Truth is, when you have read this book you will experience the delight that comes from knowing before there was Jesse Ventura, there was Roy Wilkins leading the fight for civil rights. You will see that Dan Flynn has compiled pictures and stories of people who make us proud, who make the whole country proud. You will learn things you didn't know, and every page turned and every life revealed will, in fact, make you feel better. He has published a remarkable history of our times, and Dan Flynn's mom and dad would be proud. He's done something wonderful, by shining the light on other people. Other people, I might add, from home.

— Don Shelby

Acknowledgements

I AM VERY GRATEFUL TO A THOSE PEOPLE who have helped me make this book a reality. My parents Terry and Kathy Flynn lent their insight to my early drafts. My brothers and sisters and their families were very supportive. To Jack, who is one of my nephews, and wants me to visit him at school and explain to his classmates why it took so long to write this book, thanks for caring. My beloved Jayne, thank you for helping with the typing and for looking over some of the drafts.

To my design person Julie Tilka, thank you for your enduring patience. Also, to Kristal Leebrick, thank you for your guidance as a copy editor. My brother Vince Flynn requested that I keep him off the list of Famous Minnesotans. He did, however, encourage me. Thank you Vince.

Ross Bernstein, the hardest working author in Minnesota, introduced me to his publisher Norton Stillman. That was a class move. Thank you Ross. My gratitude continues. John Toren, thank you for your patience, and Norton Stillman, thank you for believing in this book. Thank you to the following people as well: Mike Hays, Stephan Jones, Griffith Jones, Kristina Clark, Rob Hansen, Molly Malone, Sameth Overton, Mike Holetz, Sandy Rappaport, Chris Longley, Roger Mann, Virginia Brown, Craig Wright, Fred Dahl, Ali Salem, Don Leper, David Tripp, Jody Hoffman, the Drahos Family, Sally Brewer, Dan Bliven, Dave Norris, Doneta Hoffman, Cindy Rae, Paul Bergly, Jimmy Erickson, Don Shelby, Rick Ouellette and Kelly Pratt of the Minnesota Film Board, and Bonnie Wilson and her staff at the Minnesota Historical Society.

Introduction

FOR AS LONG AS I CAN REMEMBER, I have enjoyed reading about the lives of famous people and the ways they overcame adversity to do things that had never been done before. In the course of my reading I began to notice that some of the individuals whom I truly admired were Minnesotans, either by birth or by choice, and somewhere along the way it occurred to me that it would be interesting to gather their stories together.

Minnesota may seem like just another piece of "fly-over land," tucked against the Canadian border and vanishing into the Great Plains, to those who are unfamiliar with its people and culture. Yet the state is remarkable in many ways, not least being the surprising number of prominent individuals who were born and raised here, or who made their mark within its environs. Mary Tyler Moore is not from Minnesota, and Mary Richards never actually existed (although there is a statue in her honor on Nicollet Mall in downtown Minneapolis) but the creator of the Peanuts comic strip, the inventor of Post-It Notes, the father of open-heart surgery, and America's first recipient of the Nobel Prize for Literature all made Minnesota their home. Presidential candidates, World Series heroes, film stars, Antarctic pioneers—Minnesota has produced them all, and you'll read their stories here.

Perhaps there should be a walk of fame on Nicollet Mall, with stars bearing the names of well-known Minnesotans—actress Jessica Lange, novelist John Sanford, music producers Jimmy Jam Harris and Terry Lewis, Ojibwe pitcher Charles Bender, humorist Garrison Keillor—running up and down its length. Until that time, we have *Famous Minnesotans*, to remind us of the creativity, intelligence, commitment to justice, and athletic prowess that has long flourished, and continues to thrive, within our fine state.

— Dan Flynn

JUDY GARLAND

PIGSKIN PARADE

(1936) Thirteen-year-old Judy Garland makes her voice memorable in this musical about a Texas pumpkin-throwing football player who leads his team to the Yale Bowl.

THE WIZARD OF OZ

(1939) Garland plays a Kansas farm girl who is taken by a tornado to a fantasy land. A special Oscar (underage) is given to Garland for her portrayal of Dorothy Gale.

MEET ME IN ST. LOUIS

(1944) In this Vincente Minnelli musical, Garland's father is a banker who is considering moving his family to New York from St. Louis. Judy sings, "Have Yourself a Merry Little Christmas."

THE CLOCK

(1945) Garland meets a G.I. under the clock at New York's mammoth Pennsylvania Station, and she falls in love. It was directed by Vincente Minnelli.

JUDGMENT AT NUREMBERG

(1961) Garland receives an Oscar nomination for her role as Irene Hoffman, who had been accused of associating with a Jew. This drama about a Nazi war-crimes trial is superbly acted. Abby Mann's screenplay won an Oscar.

THE ACTORS

Judy Garland

FRANCES GUMM, WHO LATER became Judy Garland, began her singing career at the age of two and a half, singing "Jingle Bells" to a holiday crowd at her parents' movie theater in Grand Rapids, Minnesota. The family later moved to the West Coast, and Frances performed a vaudeville routine along with her two older sisters. Audiences loved the singing, but the girls' name—the Gumm Sisters—often drew guffaws, and before long Frances Gumm had changed hers to Judy Garland.

Garland signed a contract with Metro-Goldwyn-Mayer when she was thirteen. The starlet made four films with MGM before being cast as Dorothy Gale in *The Wizard of Oz*, for which performance she won a special Oscar at the 1939 Academy Awards.

Following her success in *The Wizard of Oz*, Garland was given starring roles in *Babes in Arms*, *Meet Me in St. Louis*, and *Easter Parade*, along with numerous lesser films, but by the end of the decade the pace of work and the pressures of the studio system had undermined her health, and a studio-enforced regimen of pep pills only added to her utter exhaustion. Tired and professionally unstable, Garland was removed from the starring role of two films, *The Barkleys of Broadway* and *Annie Get Your Gun*, and hospitalized several times.

Once she had returned to health Garland continued her career by delivering successful stage shows in London and New York. She was called back to Hollywood in 1954 to work with director George Cukor in *A Star is Born*, a film that showcased both her singing and acting talents to full effect. The film recounts a few years in the life of an aging and washed-up actor (played by James Mason) and his beautiful young wife (played by Garland), whose career is just beginning to take off. Garland's vigor and compassion saved the film from bathos, and she also lent financial support to the lavish production, but it was shortened mercilessly before release, and it did little to erase her reputation as an unstable and unreliable actress.

The remainder of Garland's career was devoted largely to stage shows and popular recordings. From 1962 to 1964 she hosted *The Judy Garland Show* on CBS television. It drew critical raves but had the misfortune to be slotted on Sunday nights opposite the wildly popular show *Bonanza*. After her show was cancelled Garland continued to tour regularly, but problems with drugs and alcohol persisted, and she died in June 1969 of an accidental overdose at the age of forty-seven.

Following her success in *The Wizard of Oz*, Garland was given starring roles in *Babes in Arms*, *Meet Me in St. Louis*, and *Easter Parade*, along with numerous lesser films.

LEA THOMPSON HAS APPEARED in more than seventeen films and was the star of the popular television sitcom *Caroline in the City* in the late 1990s.

She was born in Rochester, Minnesota, on May 31, 1961, and later moved to Minneapolis. Thompson graduated from Marshall-University High School at the age of sixteen. Within a year she was headed to New York to pursue a career in ballet and theater.

Thompson is an accomplished dancer and has performed in more than fifty ballets. Discouraged by Baryshnikov's judgment that she did not have the right figure for ballet, she turned to acting. Early stage credits include an appearance at the Pasadena Playhouse in *Bus Stop* and at the Los Angeles Theatre Center in *The Illusion*. She first made a splash on the big screen playing Lorraine McFly in *Back to the Future* (1985). Several other screen roles followed, before Thompson accepted the lead role in the TV series *Caroline in the City*.

Thompson recently starred in the Lifetime series *For the People* as a liberal chief deputy district attorney in Los Angeles.

Thompson is married to director Howard Deutch. They have two children and live in San Fernando Valley, California.

Lea Thompson is an accomplished dancer and has performed in more than fifty ballets. Discouraged by Mikhail Baryshnikov's judgment that she did not have the right figure for ballet, she turned to acting.

Lea Thompson

Kevin Sorbo

BORN IN MOUND, MINNESOTA, Sorbo graduated from Mound West Tonka High School in 1976 and studied marketing at the University of Minnesota and Moorhead State University before dropping out to pursue a modeling career in Europe. A few years later he moved to Los Angeles, where he supported himself doing commercials and television pilots, and also appeared in community theater. Sorbo was considered, but eventually passed over, for the lead roles in both *The X-Files* and *Lois and Clark: The New Adventures of Superman*, but he hit pay-dirt when he was chosen for the lead role in *Hercules: The Legendary Journeys*. Filmed on location in New Zealand, the show was a great success, with over four million American viewers, and was broadcast overseas in forty-seven countries.

In 1997 Sorbo starred in his first feature film, *Kull the Conqueror*, and he also made guest appearances in numerous television shows, including *Dharma & Greg*, *Just Shoot Me*, and *Murder, She Wrote*. The relative isolation of its New Zealand location drove Sorbo to relinquish his commitment to *Hercules* in 1999. Not long afterward he became involved in both acting and directing *Andromeda*, a science fiction television show. The show also became successful and was syndicated in seventy-eight countries.

Josh Hartnett

JOSH HARTNETT WAS BORN in San Francisco on July 28, 1978. His family later moved to Minnesota. He graduated from Minneapolis South High School and went on to attend SUNY in Purchase, New York. After appearing on the television show *Crackers*, Hartnett acted in plays and made commercials before making his motion picture debut in *Halloween: H_2O* (1998). Other roles followed, and his portrayal of an elite U.S. Army Ranger in *Black Hawk Down* (2001) brought rave reviews from the critics. By age twenty-two, Hartnett had hosted the NBC television show *Saturday Night Live*, introduced a film segment at the 2002 Academy Awards, and starred alongside Harrison Ford in the buddy cop film *Hollywood Homicide*.

Hartnett's recent credits include *40 Days and 40 Nights* (2002) and *Wicker Park* (2004).

The low-keyed Hartnett often returns to Minneapolis and enjoys spending his summers here.

By age twenty-two, Josh Hartnett had hosted the NBC television show *Saturday Night Live*, introduced a film segment at the 2002 Academy Awards, and starred alongside Harrison Ford in the buddy cop film *Hollywood Homicide*.

RACHAEL LEIGH COOK WAS MODELING by age ten, and her parents allowed her to move to California alone to pursue an acting career when she was a young teen. Born on October 4, 1979, she spent her early years in Bloomington, Minnesota. Cook appeared in print ads for Target stores before taking up acting. She performed in school musicals as well. With her parents' encouragement she worked toward becoming an actor. The breakthrough came with her appearance in a thirty-second anti-drug commercial.

In 1995, not long after moving west, Cook nailed her first audition, snaring a prominent role in *The Baby-Sitters Club*. *The House of Yes* (1997) followed, and with *She's All That* (1999) Cook solidified her presence among the teen acting elite. She was even compared to Audrey Hepburn for her portrayal in that film of Laney Boggs, a hapless youth who is transformed from an ugly duckling into the most popular girl in school. She won the Blockbuster Favorite Newcomer Award for the performance.

Certainly one of the most sought after talents of her generation, Cook appeared on the cover of *Entertainment Weekly* for her starring role in *Josie and the Pussycats* (2001). *All I Wanna Do* (1998), *Blow Dry* (2001), and *Tangled* (2001) are only a few of the many films she's appeared in since turning twenty.

Rachel Lee Cook has appeared in over thirty films in all, among them *The Big Empty* (2003) and *Texas Rangers* (2001), and she starred recently in the made-for-television film *Fearless*.

The stunning young actress lives in Los Angeles. Mom and Dad as well as younger brother Ben await her return visits to Minnesota.

Rachael Leigh Cook

Al Franken

AL FRANKEN WAS BORN IN 1951 in New York City but grew up in St. Louis Park, Minnesota. He began writing parodies and satires of classroom activities in the second grade. As a teen he performed in local comedy clubs with friend Tom Davis.

By the time he graduated from Harvard University in 1973, Franken's imagination had been fertilized by exposure to the work of Dick Gregory, Godfrey Cambridge, and Lenny Bruce, and he soon landed a job (once again with Davis) writing comedy skits for the Not Ready for Prime Time Players on the television show *Saturday Night Live*. The show's cast included John Belushi, Chevy Chase, Gilda Radner, Bill Murray, Jane Curtin, and Dan Ackroyd, among many others. Franken was with the show from 1975 to 1980, and then again from 1985 to 1995, and he won four Emmys for collaborative comedy writing during that time. He acted on the show as well, most memorably as the fatuous self-help guru Stuart Smalley.

He was widely praised for his coverage of the 1992 presidential campaigns on Comedy Central's *Indecision '92*, and his performance at the 1994 White House Correspondents Dinner placed him in great demand as a guest speaker.

Franken's interest in self-help programs, which he parodied successfully in *I'm Good Enough, I'm Smart Enough, and Doggone It, People Like Me* (1992), took a more serious turn in the film *When a Man Loves a Woman* (1994), a sober-minded look at alcohol abuse starring Meg Ryan, which he cowrote. His flair for satire also took on added dimension in two books aimed at the deceit of right-wing journalists: *Rush Limbaugh is a Big Fat Idiot* (1996), and the recent *New York Times* bestseller *Lies and the Lying Liars Who Tell Them: A Fair and Balanced Look at the Right* (2003).

Franken recently became the host of a daily liberal radio show, *The Al Franken Show*. He had discussed with Minnesota Democratic Party officials the possibility of running for the U.S. Senate in 2008, but eventually decided not to run.

Franken was with *Saturday Night Live* from 1975 to 1980, and then again from 1985 to 1995, and he won four Emmys for collaborative comedy writing during that time.

AL FRANKEN

SATURDAY NIGHT LIVE

(1975) Al Franken and Tom Davis write knockout material for the cutting-edge Not Ready for Prime Time Players on *Saturday Night Live*.

TRADING PLACES

(1983) Franken and Davis play Amtrak baggage handlers who become part of the New Year's Eve celebration on the train.

STUART

(1985–1995) Franken delights viewers as Stuart Smalley, a self-affirming disciple of the 12-step program.

AUTHOR/GRAMMY

(1997) Franken wins a Grammy for Best-Spoken Comedy Album, based on his best-selling book, *Rush Limbaugh is a Big Fat Idiot and Other Observations*.

OH, THE THINGS I KNOW!: A GUIDE TO SUCCESS, OR FAILING THAT, HAPPINESS

(2001) In this number-one best seller, Franken makes fun of advice books.

LewAyres

LEW AYRES WAS BORN in Minneapolis in 1908, and attended West High School. After the family moved to California, Ayres formed a swing band with some friends. One night during a performance he was discovered by an agent, and not long afterward he was cast opposite Greta Garbo in the silent film *The Kiss* (1929). The next year he starred in *All Quiet on the Western Front*, an experience that changed his life. The film won the Best Picture Oscar for 1930, and the young, handsome actor received excellent reviews for his portrayal of the boyish German soldier Paul Baumer.

All the same, Ayres's career floundered during the thirties, and he did not return to fame and fortune until he landed the lead in the medical series *Dr. Kildare* (1939–1942). But the experience of making the antiwar *All Quiet on the Western Front* had left its mark, and when the United States entered World War II Ayres applied for conscientious objector status. The public was shocked, and they boycotted his films for years. It was only after being decorated several times as a medical orderly in the Pacific theatre that Ayres's reputation was rehabilitated in Hollywood.

Ayres later appeared in several other films, most notably as a doctor in *Jonny Belinda*, for which he received an Oscar nomination; and he was offered the lead in the *Dr. Kildare* television series. Ayres requested that the studio prohibit cigarette advertisements from airing during the show, and when they refused to do so, the principled actor declined the part.

He died in 1996 in Los Angeles.

JANE RUSSELL WAS BORN June 21, 1921, in Bemidji, Minnesota. She first became famous as a result of her presence, if not her performance, in Howard Hughes' film *The Outlaw*, which was withheld from distribution for many years because of suggestive content. It was made in 1940, but was not widely seen until 1946 after a lengthy battle with the censors. In later films Russell revealed more than mere anatomy, however, charming viewers in two comedies with Bob Hope, *The Paleface* and *Son of Paleface*, and in the Howard Hawks extravaganza, *Gentlemen Prefer Blondes*. Russell appeared in more than twenty-five films in all, and remained in the public eye in later life as the full-figured woman in Maidenform bra commercials.

In 1950 Russell started the World Adoption International Fund (WAIF), an organization that has helped place over 38,000 orphaned and foster care children into adoptive homes.

Jane Russell

AS THE OPENING CREDITS rolled for the 1970s sitcom *Happy Days*, with Bill Haley and the Comets rocking around the clock, a smiling Marion Ross appeared on the screen as Mrs. Cunningham, the matriarch of a fictional small-town family. The Albert Lea native became a household name while working with Ron Howard, Henry Winkler, Penny Marshall, and the other regulars on that show, in which family life during the 1950s was marvelously depicted. Ross was as funny as anyone in the cast.

Ross grew up in Minneapolis and later attended San Diego State College in California, where she was named the school's outstanding actress. After taking classes and appearing in plays, Ross eventually landed parts in several movies, most notably *The Glenn Miller Story* (1954), *Sabrina* (1954), and *Operation Petticoat* (1959).

She received two Emmy nominations for her role on *Happy Days* and went on to appear on several episodes of *Loveboat*, as well as on Broadway in the play *Arsenic and Old Lace*. Ross also received two Emmy nominations for her work in the television show *Brooklyn Bridge* (1991–1993), playing Sophie Berger, a Jewish grandmother in 1950s Brooklyn.

Ross was nominated for a Golden Globe award for her portrayal of Rosie Dunlap in the movie *The Evening Star*. The celebrated actress also received two Emmy nominations for Notable Guest Appearances on *The Drew Carey Show* (1997) and *Touched by an Angel*. A consummate professional, Ross continues to star in movies, including *Ladies and the Champ* (2001), in which she and Olympia Dukakis play two grandmothers who train a street kid to become a prizefighter. The prolific actress can also be heard in *SpongeBob SquarePants* (2002) as the voice of Grandma SquarePants.

Ross currently lives in San Fernando Valley, California.

Marion Ross